A Trip to Camp Danger

Happy House

About Wise & Wide

- A systematic 6-level English reading program based on Lexile® measures
- Diverse and interesting topics chosen from the elementary curriculums of Korea and English speaking western countries
- Well-written books in various forms including fiction stories, descriptive texts, and classics retold
- The informative but original fiction stories grab your interest, leading to the easy and clear understanding of the educational content.
- Improve thinking skills with solid after-reading activities at all levels of the series.

Wise & Wide is a 6-level English reading program that consists of 60 books and each level is systematically divided by Lexile® measures. The Lexile® Framework for Reading is the most popular reading measuring system in American formal education curriculums and many English programs. Over 20 out of 50 states in the U.S. mark Lexile® measures directly on students' final report cards and over 300 well-known publishers adopt and use Lexile® measures.

Experience many kinds of readings written by professional writers from the U.S. and England. They used interesting topics that were carefully chosen after analyzing elementary curriculums from around the world including Korea, the U.S., England, and Australia among many others. Comprehensive after-reading activities including graphic organizers, speaking tasks, and After-reading Tests are ready for you.

Levels in the series and their corresponding Lexile® measures

Level	Lexile® measures	U.S. Grade
Level 1	Below 200L	Pre K - K
Level 2	190L - 400L	Lower Grade 1
Level 3	350L - 530L	Upper Grade 1
Level 4	420L - 650L	Grade 2
Level 5	520L - 940L	Grade 3 - 4
Level 6	830L - 1070L	Grade 5 - 6

* Smart Readers: Wise & Wide level 1 is applicable to the preschool level in the U.S.
* The source of the relationship between Lexile® measures and U.S. school grades: CCSS(Common Core State Standards) FOR ENGLISH LANGUAGE ARTS, APPENDIX A (2012, which is used by 45 states in the U.S.)

Topic List

	Level 1	Level 2	Level 3	Level 4	Level 5	Level 6
Book 1	Science>Biology: The hibernation of animals Story	Science>Biology: Living and nonliving things Story	Science>Biology> Animals & the Environment: Sea otters Story	Environment> Living with nature: The diver & the persimmon tree Story	Science>Biology> Anima : Amazing animals of the Amazon Story	Science>Biology: Germs, transmitted diseases Story
Book 2	Literature> World classics: Aesop's fables Story	Literature> Traditional fairy tale: Old tales about stones Story	Social Studies> Economy: To run a business to make and save money Story	Science>Biology> Plants: Photosynthesis Story	Science>Earth science: Earth's layers, earthquakes, volcanoes, and earth's atmosphere Report	Mathematics> Sequence: The golden ratio & the Fibonacci sequence Story
Book 3	Science>Physics: How shadows are formed Story	Literature> World classics: Peter Pan Story	Science>Scientific technology: Nanobots Story	Literature>Myths: World's creation stories Story	Literature> Legend: The story of King Arthur Story	
Book 4	Literature> Traditional literature: The Talmud Story	Science>Biology> Animal: Polar bears Story	Science>Biology> Animal: Mountain gorillas Story	Social Studies> Cultural anthropology: Amazing ancient cultures of the world Story	Science> Earth science: Clouds and weather Story	
Book 5			Social Studies> Cultural anthropology: Astonishing festivals Report	Art>Music: Stories from two operas Story		
Book 6				Social Studies> People: Three great people who overcame hardships Story		
Book 7						
Book 8						
Book 9						
Book 10						

* 10 books in each level will be published.

How to Use
This Book

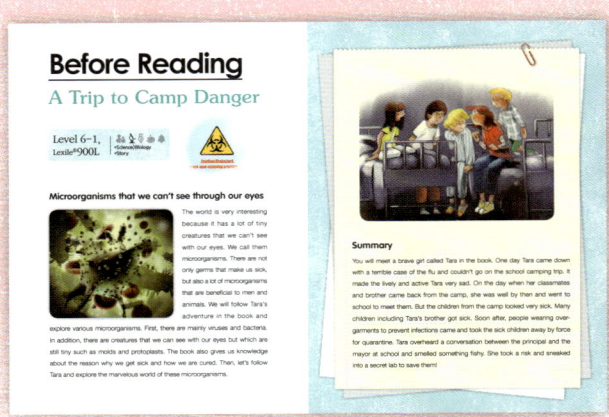

•Before Reading

You can easily find the topic and what kind of story you are about to read.

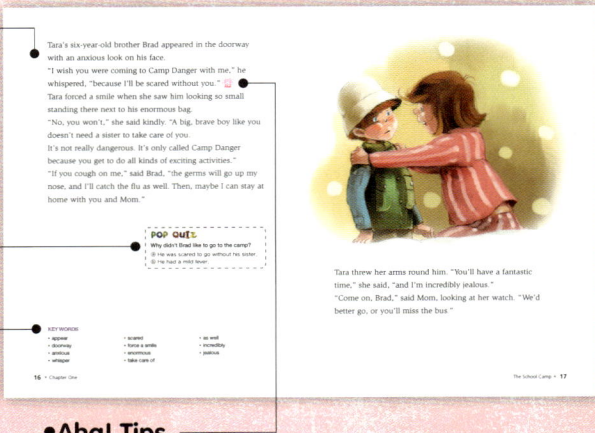

•The text

All the stories were written by professional writers from the U.S. and England, so you will read authentic and appropriate English sentences and expressions in every book in the series.

•Pop Quiz

Check out right away if you understand what you have just read by solving a pop quiz that checks your comprehension.

•Key Words

The key words and expressions on each page are listed for you to easily study them.

•Aha! Tips

Download free Korean explanations at *www.ihappyhouse.co.kr* for all of the sentences marked with "Aha!". These explain cultural, scientific, and economic knowledge or they deal with aspects of English such as grammatical structures or idiomatic expressions. There are lots of "Aha! Tips" to help you understand the text.

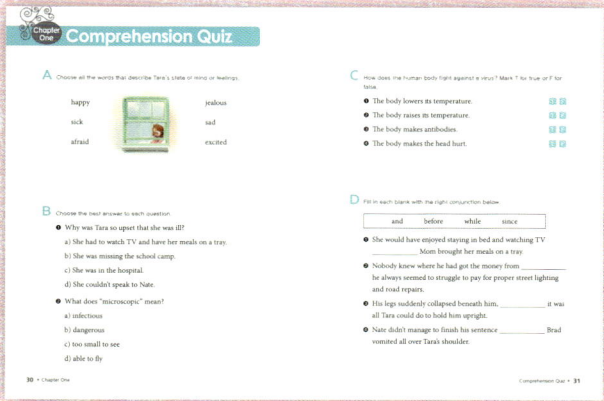

•Comprehension Quiz

After reading one chapter, solve various questions to find out if you fully understand the content.

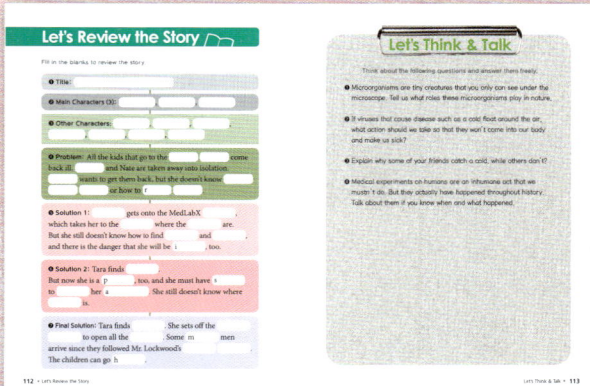

•Let's Review the Story /
•Let's Think & Talk

Fill in the blanks in the organizer to summarize the whole story. Express your own thinking and feelings about the story by answering the questions. You can build up logic and reasoning skills for your essay examinations in the future.

Appendix

Audio CD
In the CD audio book form, the texts are read vividly by American professional voice actors.

After-reading Test
Solve an additionally provided After-reading Test for each book.

The Korean translation, Answer Keys, a Word Quiz, a Word List, and
Aha! Tips for each book
You can download them for free at *www.ihappyhouse.co.kr*

Before Reading

A Trip to Camp Danger

Level 6-1,
Lexile® 900L

•Science>Biology
•Story

Caution:Biohazard.
u are now entering a restric

Microorganisms that we can't see through our eyes

The world is very interesting because it has a lot of tiny creatures that we can't see with our eyes. We call them microorganisms. There are not only germs that make us sick, but also a lot of microorganisms that are beneficial to men and animals. We will follow Tara's adventure in the book and explore various microorganisms. First, there are mainly viruses and bacteria. In addition, there are creatures that we can see with our eyes but which are still tiny such as molds and protoplasts. The book also gives us knowledge about the reason why we get sick and how we are cured. Then, let's follow Tara and explore the marvelous world of these microorganisms.

Summary

You will meet a brave girl called Tara in the book. One day Tara came down with a terrible case of the flu and couldn't go on the school camping trip. It made the lively and active Tara very sad. On the day when her classmates and brother came back from the camp, she was well by then and went to school to meet them. But the children from the camp looked very sick. Many children including Tara's brother got sick. Soon after, people wearing over-garments to prevent infections came and took the sick children away by force for quarantine. Tara overheard a conversation between the principal and the mayor at school and smelled something fishy. She took a risk and sneaked into a secret lab to save them!

Contents

A Trip to Camp Danger

A Trip to Camp Danger

The School Camp

Tara struggled to a sitting position in the bed so that she could see out the window. A cough shook her until her ribs ached, and her head began to hurt as she thought, for the millionth time, how unfair it was that she had to catch the flu this week, of all weeks. If it had been an ordinary school week, she wouldn't have minded.

In fact, she would have enjoyed staying in bed and watching TV while Mom brought her meals on a tray. But this was the week she had been looking forward to for months, ever since the school principal, Mr. Lockwood, had first announced the trip to Camp Danger.

KEY WORDS

- struggle
- rib
- cough
- shake (shake-shook-shaken)
- ache
- for the millionth time

- unfair
- catch the flu
- of all
- mind
- look forward to
- principal

- announce
- bedside table
- fever
- manage

"Are you all right, sweetheart?" Mom came in with a tall glass of orange juice and put it down on the bedside table. "How's your fever this morning? Do you think you can manage some breakfast?"

POP QUIZ

Where does the opening scene take place?
ⓐ a hospital
ⓑ a bedroom

Mom laid a cool hand on Tara's forehead and said, "You still feel very hot. Your temperature must be high."

Tara groaned and pressed her forehead against the cool glass of the window. "Why does having the flu make me so hot?"

"The high temperature is your body's way of killing germs," explained Mom.

"Most of the viruses or bacteria that like to live in the human body can only survive at around thirty-seven degrees Celsius, which is the normal temperature of a healthy human. Your brain tells your body to get just hot enough to kill the virus without damaging you!"

Tara imagined the flu virus invading her body and attacking her cells like tiny, spiky bombs and her body fighting back, heating itself up to kill its enemies, and producing antibodies—those special proteins that acted like an army—to destroy the germs.

"It's not fair," she groaned. "I wanted to go climbing and swimming and to do all those other exciting things they'll be doing at camp. Yet here I am, stuck in bed while the whole school goes away for a week—everyone except me."

KEY WORDS

- virus
- bacteria
- survive
- Celsius
- damage
- invade
- spiky
- heat up
- antibody
- stuck in

"Hey, Tara!" came a familiar voice drifting through the open window.

It was Nate, Tara's best friend, grinning up at her and lifting his hand to shield his eyes from the morning sun.

"How are you feeling?" he called.

"Hot as an oven," she shouted back.

Nate looked upset as he pushed his blond hair back from his face. "That doesn't sound good. I'm really sorry, but I've got to go, or I'll miss the bus." 📖 Aha!

Tara blinked hard to hold back the sudden tears that pricked her eyes as he waved and ran off.

"It won't be the same here without you, Nate," she murmured. "I'll be the only school-age kid left in town."

It was true. For the first time, the entire school was going to the camp, which was paid for by the mayor of the town. Nobody knew where he had got the money from, since he always seemed to struggle to pay for proper street lighting and road repairs.

KEY WORDS

- familiar
- drift
- grin up at
- shield
- blink

- **hold back** (hold-held-held)
- **prick**
- **run off** (run-ran-run)
- **murmur**
- **for the first time**

- **pay for**
- **mayor**
- **town**
- **repair**

Tara's six-year-old brother Brad appeared in the doorway with an anxious look on his face.

"I wish you were coming to Camp Danger with me," he whispered, "because I'll be scared without you." 📖 Aha!

Tara forced a smile when she saw him looking so small standing there next to his enormous bag.

"No, you won't," she said kindly. "A big, brave boy like you doesn't need a sister to take care of you.

It's not really dangerous. It's only called Camp Danger because you get to do all kinds of exciting activities."

"If you cough on me," said Brad, "the germs will go up my nose, and I'll catch the flu as well. Then, maybe I can stay at home with you and Mom."

POP QUIZ

Why didn't Brad like to go to the camp?
ⓐ He was scared to go without his sister.
ⓑ He had a mild fever.

KEY WORDS

- appear
- doorway
- anxious
- whisper
- scared
- force a smile
- enormous
- take care of
- as well
- incredibly
- jealous

Tara threw her arms round him. "You'll have a fantastic time," she said, "and I'm incredibly jealous."

"Come on, Brad," said Mom, looking at her watch. "We'd better go, or you'll miss the bus."

By the end of the week, Tara felt well enough to run down to school to meet the returning buses.

"Did you all have an amazing time?" she asked, as all the kids, looking dirty and exhausted, tumbled off.

That was normal, since nobody took a shower on school trips, nor did they get much sleep. But beneath the layer of dirt, some of the pupils looked strangely pale, and one of the younger kids vomited as soon as he stepped off the bus. Travel sickness, most likely, Tara guessed. Her eyes darted this way and that as she looked through the crowd for Brad or Nate.

Mr. Lockwood, who had insisted on staying behind to catch up with some work, came hurrying out of the school. He had a horrified look on his face as he took in the scene. He was mumbling something under his breath, and as he passed Tara, she caught the words *never thought it would be this bad*.

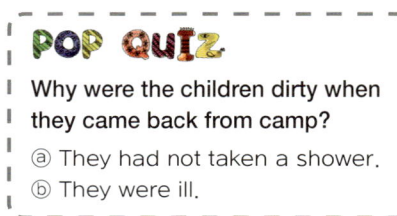

POP QUIZ

Why were the children dirty when they came back from camp?

ⓐ They had not taken a shower.
ⓑ They were ill.

KEY WORDS

- amazing
- exhausted
- tumble off
- beneath
- layer
- dirt
- pupil
- pale
- vomit
- step off

KEY WORDS

- travel sickness
- most likely
- dart
- look through
- insist on
- catch up with
- come hurrying
- horrified
- take in
- scene
- mumble
- under one's breath

The School Camp • **19**

Tara tried to hear more, but was distracted when she suddenly spotted Brad's flame-colored hair. The moment he saw her, he burst into tears and fell into her arms.

"It's okay," she murmured as she kissed the top of his head, which still smelled faintly of shampoo despite his unwashed hair.

He pressed himself against her and whispered, "I don't feel too well."

"Hey, what's this?" gasped Tara, grabbing Brad's arm, which was covered with tiny red dots that formed a rash all the way down to the backs of his hands.

His legs suddenly collapsed beneath him, and it was all Tara could do to hold him upright.

"Come on, buddy," she whispered into his hair. "I think you've got something worse than the flu."

She heaved him onto her back and told him to hold on tight.

"Tara!" called a voice, and there was Nate, pushing his way through the crowd toward her.

"You're lucky you didn't go on that trip because loads of people got sick, although I seem to have avoided it somehow. Camp Danger was the right name for it!"

His eyes glanced toward Brad in concern. "You'd better get him home. He doesn't look too..."

Nate didn't manage to finish his sentence before Brad vomited all over Tara's shoulder.

POP QUIZ

Why did Nate tell Tara that she was lucky?
ⓐ Many students at the camp got sick.
ⓑ The camp was boring.

KEY WORDS

- distracted
- spot
- flame-colored
- burst into
- faintly
- despite

- grab (grab-grabbed-grabbed)
- dot
- rash
- all the way down
- collapse
- upright

- heave
- hold on
- push one's way through
- loads of
- glance
- in concern

When Tara returned to school on Monday, at least one third of the kids were absent as they had come down with the strange sickness. By Wednesday, the classes were half empty, and the corridors echoed with silence.

"What's going on?" whispered Tara as she and Nate sat at the back of the class, surrounded by empty chairs.

Even the teacher, Miss Carter, sat at her desk with her head in her hands. She looked half asleep and her normally creamy, smooth skin was covered with scarlet dots. Aha!

"I... I think I need to go home," she whispered before collapsing onto the desk as her eyes rolled back in her head. Tara leapt up, her heart hammering as fear tightened her chest. She didn't need a teacher to tell her that something was wrong here—seriously wrong. Nate was already on his feet and halfway out the door to fetch Mr. Lockwood.

"Nate!" she called after him, but she broke off as a boy sitting by the window slowly slithered to the floor.

KEY WORDS

- at least
- come down with
- corridor
- echo
- surround

- creamy
- be covered with
- scarlet
- leap up (leap-leapt-leapt)
- hammer

- chest
- be on one's feet
- fetch
- break off (break-broke-broken)
- slither

Tara hesitated, swinging her weight uncertainly from one foot to the other. Should she go and help him? But what if she caught something from him? Whatever this disease was, there was no doubt it was highly infectious.

She imagined the microscopic particles hovering in a cloud around her head, waiting for her to breathe them in. _Aha!_ She pressed her hands over her nose and mouth to protect them from whatever might be hanging in the air. But what about the desks or the door handle? What about the books, chairs, pens, and pencils?

> ## POP QUIZ
> Why didn't Tara go to help the boy in her class?
> ⓐ She didn't like him.
> ⓑ She was afraid of being infected.

KEY WORDS

- hesitate
- swing
- weight
- infectious
- microscopic

- particle
- hover
- be infected with
- disease
- crash

- wipe
- bald
- mutter
- anxious

Miss Carter surely must have touched them, and the germs might have been on her hands, which meant that now Tara had touched them, too. Her own fingers might be infected with the disease.

Unable to stand still a moment longer, she hurried out of the classroom and into the corridor, where she almost crashed into Nate. Mr. Lockwood was directly behind Nate. He wiped his broad, bald head with a large handkerchief.
"I don't know what to do," Mr. Lockwood muttered. "If I'd known, I never would have agreed…"
Tara had never seen him look so anxious.
"Go home," he said, "and stay there until you hear from the education department. I'm closing the school."

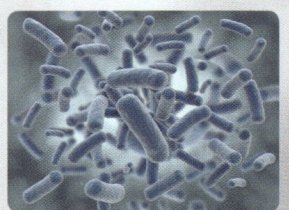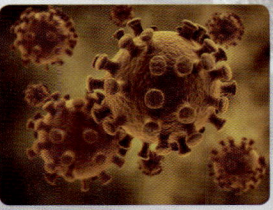

▲ Viruses are found wherever there is life.

It was a humid night and Tara tossed and turned restlessly in her bed. Unable to sleep, she drifted in and out of dreams. She only came fully awake when she realized that someone was moaning softly in the room next door. She flung back the bed covers and padded across the corridor to see what was happening.

Brad lay in the sheets. His eyes were wide and unseeing, and he was staring at the corner of the room as though something was there.

"Brad?" Tara whispered as she crouched beside him and laid a hand on his forehead.

His skin was so hot she could barely touch it.

"Mom?" she called, but before anyone had time to answer, there was a loud hammering at the front door.

"Open up!" yelled a harsh male voice. "We need to enter this property."

POP QUIZ

What does "to toss and turn" mean?
ⓐ make a bed
ⓑ not sleep well

KEY WORDS

- humid
- toss and turn
- restlessly
- drift

- moan
- fling (fling-flung-flung)
- pad (pad-padded-padded)
- lie (lie-lay-lain)

- unseeing
- crouch
- barely
- property

KEY WORDS

- instantly
- fall down
- in one's haste
- clutch

- bathrobe
- stride
- equipment
- horrible

- alien
- gigantic
- case
- muffle

Dad was out of bed instantly, almost falling down the stairs in his haste. Mom came out of her room too, clutching her bathrobe around her. Her eyes were dark and anxious against her pale skin.

Two men came striding up the stairs. 📖 They were wearing strange white suits that covered them from head to toe, masks that covered their eyes, and some kind of breathing equipment over their nose and mouth. They looked like horrible aliens or gigantic insects.

"We believe you have a case of infection here," one of them said. His voice was muffled by the mask.

Comprehension Quiz

A Choose all the words that describe Tara's state of mind or feelings.

happy   jealous

sick   sad

afraid   excited

B Choose the best answer to each question.

❶ Why was Tara so upset that she was ill?

a) She had to watch TV and have her meals on a tray.

b) She was missing the school camp.

c) She was in the hospital.

d) She couldn't speak to Nate.

❷ What does "microscopic" mean?

a) infectious

b) dangerous

c) too small to see

d) able to fly

C How does the human body fight against a virus? Mark T for true or F for false.

❶ The body lowers its temperature. T F

❷ The body raises its temperature. T F

❸ The body makes antibodies. T F

❹ The body makes the head hurt. T F

D Fill in each blank with the right conjunction below.

and	before	while	since

❶ She would have enjoyed staying in bed and watching TV _____ Mom brought her meals on a tray.

❷ Nobody knew where he had got the money from _____ he always seemed to struggle to pay for proper street lighting and road repairs.

❸ His legs suddenly collapsed beneath him, _____ it was all Tara could do to hold him upright.

❹ Nate didn't manage to finish his sentence _____ Brad vomited all over Tara's shoulder.

Left Behind

"Do you mean Brad?" said Tara. She was hardly able to get the words out since her voice seemed to be knotted up in her throat.

The second man looked at a clipboard with some writing on it and said, "That is correct. We are authorized to remove and isolate Bradley Zuckerman, aged six years."

"No," said Mom as she backed away toward Brad's bedroom. "You're not taking him anywhere."

"What does 'isolate' mean?" whimpered Tara as the sweat on her skin cooled to ice.

KEY WORDS

- **knot up** (knot-knotted-knotted)
- **clipboard**
- **be authorized to**
- **remove**
- **isolate**
- **back away**
- **whimper**
- **cool**
- **take away**
- **rise** (rise-rose-risen)
- **shriek**

"It means they want to take him somewhere away from everyone else while he's sick," explained Dad.

"That way, nobody else can catch the illness from him."

Mom's voice rose like the siren on a police car as she shrieked again, "I said you're *not* taking him!"

Mom moved quickly into the bedroom and sat on Brad's bed with her arms wrapped tightly around him while Dad pressed both hands against the second man's chest and tried to shove him against the wall. But he was too strong, and Dad was the one who ended up lying in a heap on the floor as he groaned and rubbed his head.

"All children who attended the school camp have come into contact with a dangerous biological hazard," said the first man, reading from his clipboard. "I am authorized to take your son by force."

All children who attended the school camp...

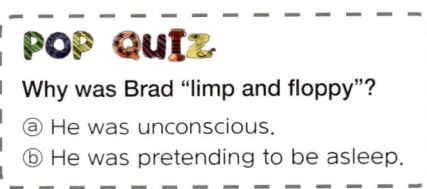

POP QUIZ

Why was Brad "limp and floppy"?

ⓐ He was unconscious.
ⓑ He was pretending to be asleep.

KEY WORDS

- **wrap** (wrap-wrapped-wrapped)
- **shove**
- **end up -ing**
- **in a heap**
- **rub**
- **come into contact with**
- **biological**

- **hazard**
- **by force**
- **squeeze**
- **hold on** (hold-held-held)
- **peel**
- **limp**
- **floppy**

- **stuffing**
- **knock out of**
- **sob**
- **tug at**
- **scoop**
- **snatch**

The two men strode over to the bed and squeezed their gloved hands around Brad's upper arms. Despite her efforts to hold on, they peeled Mom's arms from around Brad's waist and carried him toward the door. He was all limp and floppy like an old toy with all the stuffing knocked out of it. Mom ran after them. She was sobbing while tugging at their clothes and hitting their shoulders and backs.

"At least let him take his teddy," yelled Tara, scooping it from the pillow and chasing after them.

The second man hesitated just long enough to snatch it from Tara and shove it under his arm.

"*What about Nate?*" thought Tara suddenly.  "*He was at the school camp; they must have taken him, too.*" She raced down the stairs and went out the front door and around the side of the house. Then, she climbed over the backyard fence and ran as fast as she could through the trees.

At last she stopped, trembling, at the edge of Nate's yard. Tara remembered that Nate's parents were out of town, but his older brother Pete was there struggling against another pair of men.

"Get your hands off him!" roared Pete, kicking and punching.

"I'm... not... sick!" panted Nate, twisting his body to escape their grabbing hands.

But the next moment, he yelled, jerked, and fell to the ground.

"Let him go with us, or we'll deliver the full charge," threatened one of the men, waving some kind of weapon around.

KEY WORDS

- tremble
- edge
- roar
- punch
- pant
- twist
- escape
- jerk
- deliver
- charge
- threaten
- wave

Pete stepped back as the men dragged a half-conscious Nate to a white van with a sign painted on it. *MedLabX was* written in dark red letters, like blood, with a cross beneath, just like the one on the medical box Mom kept in the kitchen.

A steady stream of identical white vans passed along the road. Parents ran alongside and hammered on the sides, the hoods, and the doors, trying to stop them. Tara felt as though a weight was crushing her chest and squeezing the air out of her. Her head began to spin, and a strange buzzing sound filled her ears. It was like the time she had to have a vaccination against tetanus and she fainted when she saw the needle. Then, the sound of shouting began to fade, and darkness closed over her head.

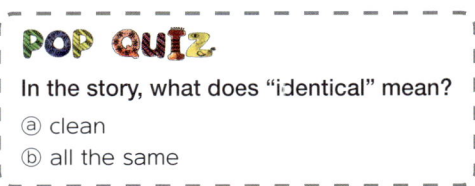

POP QUIZ

In the story, what does "identical" mean?
ⓐ clean
ⓑ all the same

KEY WORDS

- drag
- half-conscious
- steady
- stream
- identical
- alongside

- hammer
- weight
- crush
- spin
- buzzing
- vaccination

- tetanus
- faint
- fade
- close over

"Is she dead?" came a small, worried voice.

"No," muttered another voice—a woman this time, "but she's probably infectious, so don't touch her."

Tara opened her eyes and recognized Nate's neighbor from across the street. The woman jumped back and pulled the girl—who only looked about three years old—with her. Tara's lips were dry, and the first time she tried to speak, nothing came out.

"There's nothing wrong with me," she managed at last. "Have they all...?"

"They've all gone," said the woman, the final word coming out of her mouth like a bullet.

Brad was gone, Nate was gone, and so were all the other kids from school. 📖 They were gone away into isolation to keep everyone else safe. Even though she could see that keeping sick people apart from everyone made sense, there was something else that didn't make any sense at all.

"They took all the kids from the school camp, right?" she said.

But the woman was already backing away. She was clutching her daughter's hand so tightly that the girl wriggled and complained.

"So why did they take Nate," Tara called after them, "when he wasn't even ill?"

KEY WORDS

- recognize
- at last
- bullet

- isolation
- make sense
- give up -ing

- wriggle
- complain

The neighborhood was oddly quiet with no kids about. It was strange how Tara had never noticed the noise they made until it was gone. Wherever she went, people stared, obviously surprised that somebody from the school was still here.

"I didn't go to the camp," she explained at first, but after a while, she gave up trying to explain when their faces began to grow suspicious and they muttered, "Did you know something before they went?"

Two days later, the messages of hate began to appear, the first one scratched on the side of the car with a sharp blade: *You must have known.* Aha!

Then, the following day, there was one splashed all over the front door in red paint: *What's so special about your kid?*

KEY WORDS

- neighborhood
- oddly
- notice
- obviously

- suspicious
- hate (= hatred)
- scratch
- splash

- security check
- do harm

Tara went down to the school to see if anyone there could tell her any more. The yard was empty, but a light was on in Mr. Lockwood's office.

There was no need for any security checks since there were no kids here and the harm had already been done, so Tara went straight in through the front door. Then, she went down the corridor until she reached the door of the office.

Through the frosted glass, she could see the outline of two people arguing. Mr. Lockwood—recognizable by the domed outline of his head—jabbed the other in the chest with his finger.

"You *said* it would be done sensitively, so nobody would get upset," he shouted.

"But think of the money we're getting! This town is desperate for financial help, and the government has paid us generously for this inconvenience."

Tara recognized the mayor's deep, confident voice, which was familiar from the many times she had heard it at public events in the town.

"Besides," he went on, "biological warfare is a significant threat these days. The Camp Danger project will help us all eventually."

"But how can I explain that to those desperate parents out there?" demanded Mr. Lockwood, waving toward the empty streets outside. "How long will it be before our kids come home healthy?"

POP QUIZ

How did Tara recognize the two people inside?

ⓐ Mr. Lockwood   •   •   ① his voice
ⓑ the mayor   •   •   ② his outline

KEY WORDS

- frosted
- outline
- argue
- recognizable
- domed
- jab

- sensitively
- desperate
- financial
- generously
- inconvenience
- deep

- confident
- biological warfare
- significant
- demand

There was a painful silence, during which Tara could hear nothing but the thud of her own pulse in her ears. She tried to remember what she knew about biological warfare from a TV program she had seen. She remembered that it was where one country used microorganisms like viruses or bacteria to cause sickness in its enemies. But what could that possibly have to do with the school camp?

Suddenly, the door crashed open, and the mayor rushed out. When he saw Tara, he stopped dead as though he had seen a ghost and, pointing with a trembling finger, he said, "Why is she here?"

"She didn't go to the camp," snapped Mr. Lockwood. "She didn't have the procedure, so they're not interested in her." Tara's thoughts raced as she tried to figure out what on earth they were talking about. But the mayor was already striding down the corridor, leaving behind the scent of expensive aftershave.

"It's not my fault," said Mr. Lockwood, staring at Tara with a fierce expression. "I had no choice, but I intend to make things right!"

POP QUIZ

Where had Tara learned about biological warfare?

ⓐ at school
ⓑ from a TV program

KEY WORDS

- painful
- nothing but (= only)
- thud
- pulse
- microorganism
- enemy
- crash open
- rush out
- as though (= as if)

- stop dead
- snap (snap-snapped-snapped)
- procedure
- figure out
- what on earth ...?
- scent
- fierce
- expression
- intend

Mr. Lockwood looked at his wristwatch and pressed a tiny button on the side of it so that a red light came on. It was barely a dot blinking among the hairs on his wrist. Glancing up and seeing Tara's eyes upon him, he quickly pulled his jacket sleeve down to hide it.

"You didn't see anything," he told her before slamming the office door shut behind him and running after the mayor. His voice echoed down the corridor as he called, "It's too late, Mr. Mayor. I've already alerted the media, and a television reporter will be here within the hour."

Tara looked at the office door and wondered whether to go in. There was always the danger that she might get caught, but what could they possibly do that was worse than being dragged away from your family and your home?

She took a deep breath, stepped into the office, and scanned the room. She was hoping to find some clues about the *procedure*—whatever that was. But Mr. Lockwood kept his desk very tidy, and there were no loose papers or files to look through. Tara tried the drawers, but they were locked, and there was nothing in the bookcase either.

POP QUIZ

Which of these descriptions about Mr. Lockwood is true?

ⓐ He was a bold man with hairy arms.
ⓑ He was a bearded man with hairless arms.

KEY WORDS

- tiny
- come on
- blink
- glance up
- hide (hide-hid-hidden)
- slam (slam-slammed-slammed)
- echo
- wonder
- alert
- take a deep breath
- scan
- clue
- tidy
- loose
- look through
- try
- lock

Tara moved across to the computer, her fingers clumsy as she clicked on a folder labelled *School Camp.*

And there, in front of her eyes, was a file named *MedLabX.*

A complex document opened, filled with scientific language and tables of data.

There was a report about a research program to develop new vaccines by taking antibodies from people with natural immunity. *(Aha!)*

"I know what vaccines are," Tara murmured to herself.

She half smiled as she remembered Brad's screams of protest when he had to receive an injection that would protect him from diseases such as rubella and polio.

"The injection contains a small amount of the actual germs— dead or alive—so your body recognizes them in the future and makes lots of antibodies to protect you."

So far, so good. She knew that the vaccine gave you immunity against the disease, which meant that you couldn't catch it.

"So..." She frowned as she tried to figure it all out.

"Natural immunity must be when you already have the antibodies. You can't catch the disease even when the people around you have it."

KEY WORDS

- clumsy
- click
- label
- complex
- table

- research
- develop
- immunity
- protest
- injection

- rubella
- polio
- frown

The screech of tires outside the window made her jump.
A familiar white *MedLabX* van was pulling up beneath the
trees at the edge of the schoolyard. It had some kind of metal
baggage rack on the roof and a short ladder attached to the
rear doors.

Three men jumped out. This time they were dressed in
military uniforms and carrying guns. One of them stood
guard by the van. His eyes scanned this way and that while
the others moved toward the school building.

Tara dropped to her hands and knees and crawled out of the office into the empty corridor. She got to her feet and hurried back toward the school entrance.

KEY WORDS

- screech
- jump
- pull up
- edge
- baggage

- rack
- attach to
- rear
- dressed in
- stand guard

- drop to one's hands and knees
- crawl (= creep)
- get to one's feet
- hurry back
- entrance

As she crept toward the front doors, Tara heard shouts. The soldiers were forcing Mr. Lockwood into the van while the mayor was nowhere to be seen. Now Mr. Lockwood was a prisoner, too, and unable to help in any way. A plan began to form in Tara's mind. It was a plan so daring that her palms began to sweat at the thought, and she had to wipe them on the front of her jeans.

She stepped outside and resisted the urge to break into a run. They would be less likely to take any notice of her if she just strolled casually along the front of the school. Her legs felt like rubber, and her breathing came fast and shallow.  Aha! Slowly and carefully she went until she reached the line of trees at the edge of the yard, where she darted left behind the van. Nobody could see her now.

- **creep** (creep-crept-crept)
- **prisoner**
- **form**
- **daring**
- **resist**
- **urge**

- break into a run
- be less likely to
- take notice of
- stroll
- casually
- gather oneself

- tense
- roar to life
- now or never
- launch
- rung
- forward

Tara gathered herself. Her muscles tensed as though she was an athlete at the start of a race. Suddenly, the van engine roared to life. It was now or never. She launched herself at the back of the van. Her hands closed around the rungs of the ladder just as it began to move forward.

If this van was going to where Brad and Nate were, then she was going, too.

Comprehension Quiz

A Fill in each blank with the right preposition below.

into	against	through	toward	down

❶ Mom backed away _____ Brad's bedroom.

❷ She moved quickly _____ the bedroom.

❸ Dad tried to shove the man _____ the wall.

❹ Tara raced _____ the stairs.

❺ She ran as fast as she could _____ the trees.

B The following sentences are about a vaccine. Mark T for true or F for false.

❶ an injection that is given to humans   T F

❷ an injection that prevents people from catching a disease   T F

❸ an injection that is given to ill people to make
them better   T F

❹ an injection that contains a small amount of germs   T F

❺ an injection that kills people   T F

C Choose the best answer to each question.

❶ Why did Tara feel as though "a weight was crushing her chest"?

    a) She suffered from some disease.

    b) There was something on top of her.

    c) She couldn't breathe properly.

    d) Her clothes were too tight.

❷ What is biological warfare?

    a) firing germs from guns

    b) war against people and animals

    c) the use of germs to hurt people

    d) the use of animals to sniff out bombs

D In the text, the following words were used instead of "said." Circle LOUD if the word suggests a loud speaking voice, or circle QUIET if the word suggests a quiet speaking voice.

❶ whimpered   LOUD   QUIET

❷ shrieked   LOUD   QUIET

❸ yelled   LOUD   QUIET

❹ roared   LOUD   QUIET

❺ muttered   LOUD   QUIET

❻ shouted   LOUD   QUIET

❼ murmured   LOUD   QUIET

Chapter Three

Restricted Zone

Tara had been clinging to the baggage rack for what seemed like forever. In reality, she guessed that it had been around two hours. Now the sun was beginning to drop lower in the sky and was losing some of its heat.

Tara was stiff and sore. Her hands were numb from clinging on, and her eyes were gritty from the dusty wind. Just when she thought she couldn't hold on any longer, the van turned off the highway onto a narrow track. It went through an area of dense forest before emerging into a valley blocked at the far end by a mountain.

The van slowed as it drew closer to the mountain, but it seemed to be heading straight for a wall of sheer rock.

Tara felt a jolt as the van stopped and one of the soldiers got out. She pressed herself flat against the roof and prayed that he wouldn't look up and see her. Instead, he went to a fence post at the side of the track and pulled aside a bundle of ferns.

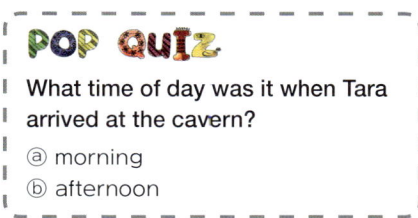

POP QUIZ

What time of day was it when Tara arrived at the cavern?

ⓐ morning
ⓑ afternoon

KEY WORDS

- cling to
- in reality
- stiff
- sore
- numb

- gritty
- track
- dense
- emerge into
- sheer

- jolt
- pull aside
- a bundle of
- fern

From where she was lying, Tara couldn't see exactly what he was doing. She heard an electronic beep, and then the rock wall shivered, groaned, and began to move. A door, cleverly disguised and invisible until now, slid open. The soldier climbed back into the van, and Tara felt a vibration right through her body as the engine roared again. The van drove through the door, and it slid down behind them and closed with a loud click.

For a moment, everything was completely black, but then a bank of lights flicked on overhead. They were in some kind of cavern, but it had been transformed into a clean, modern area like a garage, and a row of identical *MedLabX* vans was parked there.

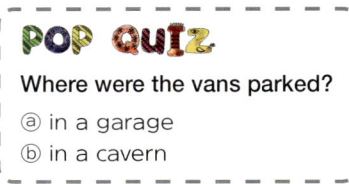

POP QUIZ

Where were the vans parked?

ⓐ in a garage
ⓑ in a cavern

KEY WORDS

- electronic
- beep
- shiver
- disguise
- invisible
- slide open (slide-slid-slid)

- drive (drive-drove-driven)
- bank
- flick on/off
- overhead
- cavern
- transform into

- hold one's breath
- hum
- machinery
- catch one's breath
- pitch darkness

Tara held her breath and waited for the shouts of discovery or for a hand to grab her legs and to drag her roughly to the ground. But there was only the sound of voices in the distance and a low background hum of machinery.

The soldiers pulled Mr. Lockwood out of the van and took him into a tunnel that opened in the wall like a black throat. Once they were gone, all the lights flicked off, and Tara was left to catch her breath in pitch darkness.

Tara stretched her aching limbs and rubbed the life back into them. Then, she climbed down off the roof and jumped onto the ground. She felt her way along the edge of the van. Her palms were flat against the cool paintwork. Confused by the darkness, she couldn't tell which way the tunnel was. But, as her eyes adjusted, she noticed a faint glow at one end of the cavern. There seemed to be a slight breeze with fresh air coming from it.

She crept toward the glow, although she stumbled a couple of times and scraped her knees on the hard, rocky floor. But the light grew stronger as she approached. Sure enough, it was the entrance to the tunnel.

She crept along it — staying low to the ground — until she emerged cautiously into a well-lit corridor with several doors in it. The walls were glaring white, and the tiled floor was so clean that it almost dazzled her to look at it. 📖 It was like a hospital. Or a laboratory.

Tara listened for signs of movement, but there was only the low murmur of voices behind closed doors. She guessed that in such a secure place, they wouldn't be expecting visitors. Even so, a tiny hum alerted her to the presence of a camera mounted on the wall and slowly moving in her direction...

KEY WORDS

- stretch
- limbs
- feel one's way
- flat
- confused
- adjust
- glow
- slight
- breeze
- stumble
- scrape
- well-lit
- glaring
- dazzle
- listen for
- secure
- presence
- mount

Tara crouched down and crawled across the corridor until she was right beneath it. Making sure that it was facing away from her, she continued toward a double door with a sign on it. Inside a yellow warning triangle was a strange black symbol: three incomplete circles joined at the center with another circle holding them all together.

Below it was a warning:

Caution: Biohazard.
You are now entering a restricted area.

Tara shivered at the thought of all the germs that must be here. A cold sweat broke out over her body, and, for a moment, she wondered whether she was already infected. But what was it Mr. Lockwood had said? *She didn't have the procedure.* Whatever was going on here, Brad and Nate were mixed up in it, and she wasn't going to leave without them. She pushed at the door, but it wouldn't open. Beside it, a keypad was mounted on the wall. As she bent closer to peer at it, there was the click of a door opening and the rapid beat of footsteps coming down the corridor behind her.

POP QUIZ
Why wouldn't the door open when Tara pushed it?
ⓐ She needed the correct code to open it.
ⓑ She needed the correct key to open it.

KEY WORDS

- make sure
- face away
- double door
- warning
- incomplete

- caution
- biohazard
- restricted
- break out
- mix up

- keypad
- bend (bend-bent-bent)
- peer at
- rapid
- beat

Without hesitating, she jumped toward the nearest door and almost fell through it into a closet for cleaning supplies. The strong smell of bleach made her feel sick, but she closed the door behind her and pressed herself against it. Her heart was beating so hard that her whole body was shaking.

There was a tap at the door, and a brisk voice demanded, "Everything all right in there?"

"Yes. Yes, sir. I'm just looking for the... the disinfectant."

The door moved as though someone was pushing on the other side.

"You can't come in," said Tara, trying to make her voice sound confident. "I've locked it for... for security reasons." Whoever was on the other side grunted, muttered something Tara couldn't hear, and moved away. Four musical-sounding beeps echoed down the corridor.

Then, there was a creaking sound, and an electronic voice announced, *"Caution; you are now entering a restricted zone."*

POP QUIZ

Why did Tara say that she was looking for disinfectant?

ⓐ She wanted to clean her hands.
ⓑ She wanted the guard to think that she belonged there.

KEY WORDS

- hesitate
- closet
- cleaning supplies
- bleach

- tap
- brisk
- disinfectant
- security

- grunt
- creak
- announce

After waiting several minutes, Tara cautiously opened the door of the cleaning cupboard and peeked out into an empty corridor. Releasing a breath she hadn't even realized she was holding, she hurried toward the keypad. She pressed a couple of keys and realized that each one had a different tone, like a musical instrument. She tried to remember the pattern of beeps she had heard. It had started at a low pitch and then risen higher.

Her fingers trembled as she stabbed at the keys. *2... 4... 6... 8.* The doors swung open, and the same electronic voice declared, *"Caution; you are now entering a restricted zone."*

POP QUIZ

What is a "microorganism"?

ⓐ a living thing that is too tiny to see with the human eye
ⓑ a small organization

KEY WORDS

- cupboard
- peek out
- release
- musical instrument
- pitch

- stab (stab-stabbed-stabbed)
- swing open (swing-swang-swung)
- declare
- lead off (lead-led-led)
- angle

- fungi
- protozoa
- stir (stir-stirred-stirred)
- be fascinated by
- microscope

Four corridors led off in different directions. Each corridor had a sign on the wall. The one immediately to her left said *Bacteria*. Directly opposite, the next corridor was *Viruses*. Then, the two others ahead that led off at angles to one another said *Fungi* and *Protozoa*.

A memory stirred in Tara's mind. They had done a study of microorganisms at school, and she had been fascinated by these tiny living things that were too small to see without a powerful microscope.

Tara knew that viruses caused the common cold as well as chicken pox and the flu, which had saved her from going to the school camp. Viruses were also responsible for more serious illnesses such as HIV and some types of meningitis. Fungal infections were generally things that occurred on the skin. They were itchy and terribly infectious, but not—as far as she knew—life threatening.

As for bacteria, there were the helpful ones in people's guts that allowed them to digest food properly. However, there were many other types that caused horrible infections in people's bodies. They ranged from the spots that the high school kids had dotted all over their faces to ones that poisoned the blood and which could kill you within hours. Tara wasn't about to go in there without a supply of strong antibiotics.

KEY WORDS

- chicken pox
- save from
- be responsible for
- serious
- HIV (= human immunodeficiency virus)
- meningitis
- fungal

- itchy
- guts (= intestines)
- range from A to B
- spot (= pimple)
- dot
- digest
- poison

- be about to
- supply
- antibiotics
- dysentery
- die of/from
- diarrhoea (= diarrhea)

But what were protozoa?  What had Miss Carter taught them about those? The memories came flooding back like a horror movie. Malaria was one disease, and there was dysentery, too — an illness that could make you die of diarrhoea. There were sleeping sicknesses, too, and other horrid diseases that you could catch from drinking infected water and which would make you vomit for days. Tara remembered Brad vomiting on her shoulder, and she began to feel ill at the thought. But if Brad was anywhere in this place, she guessed that the *Protozoa* corridor was the place to start.

▲ bacteria   ▲ fungi   ▲ protozoa

Fearful of discovery, Tara started down the corridor but retreated at once when she saw a group of white-coated scientists standing a few meters away.

"There is only a small group showing natural immunity," announced a man with a deep, booming voice, "and they will go under the anaesthetic this afternoon so that we can harvest their antibodies."

Harvesting antibodies from people with natural immunity.
That's what this program was all about, according to the file Tara had read on Mr. Lockwood's computer. She didn't know exactly what antibody harvesting was, but she didn't like the sound of anaesthetic. Anaesthetics were given to people who needed to be made unconscious, and that only happened when something unpleasant was happening to them. And this was something they wanted to do to Nate.

POP QUIZ

When might people need an anaesthetic?
ⓐ if they can't sleep at night
ⓑ if they are having surgery

KEY WORDS

- discovery
- retreat
- at once
- white-coated

- booming
- go under
- anaesthetic
- harvest

- unconscious
- unpleasant

There was the sound of footsteps scattering and the meeting breaking up. Tara stiffened, ready to run if anyone came her way, and she nervously peered around the corner.

Relieved to find that she was alone again, she tiptoed past doors with transparent panels that revealed laboratories full of scientists tapping at computers or peering at tiny tubes full of liquid. Eventually, she arrived at another door with the biohazard symbol on it; only this time, the warning was even more threatening.

Caution: Isolation area, it said, and as soon as she read the word *isolation*, she knew that this must be where they were holding the children.

Suddenly, a siren shrieked and almost split her eardrums.

KEY WORDS

- scatter
- break up
- stiffen
- nervously

- tiptoe
- transparent
- panel
- reveal

- threatening
- as soon as

"Red alert!" exclaimed the usual electronic voice with increased urgency.

"All security personnel must report to corridor D."

A hand gripped Tara's shoulder, and another twisted her arm behind her back.

"Going somewhere?" murmured a harsh voice in her ear.

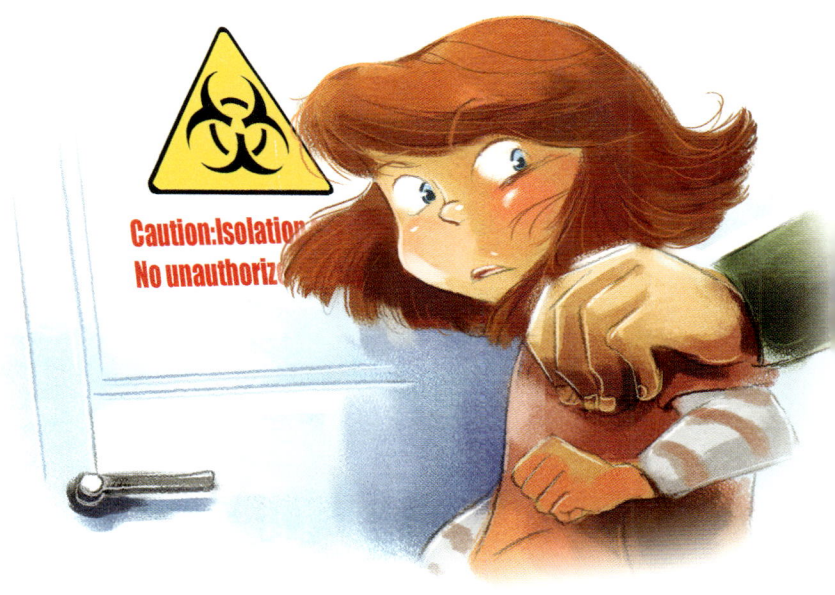

Caution: Isolation
No unauthoriz

KEY WORDS

- split
- eardrum
- alert

- exclaim
- urgency
- personnel

- grip (grip-gripped-gripped)
- twist
- harsh

A Match the two sides to make compound words.

❶ back ·   · steps

❷ paint ·   · drums

❸ key ·   · ground

❹ foot ·   · work

❺ cup ·   · board

❻ ear ·   · pad

B Choose the best answer to each question.

❶ Why did the driver pull aside the ferns?

a) They were blocking the track.

b) They were damaging the van.

c) There was a switch hidden behind them.

d) He had dropped his keys there.

❷ How are some bacteria useful to humans?

a) They help us to digest food.

b) They make antibodies.

c) They get rid of spots.

d) They destroy antibiotics.

C Fill in each blank with the right word below.

mountain	track	forest	valley

❶ The van turned down a narrow _____.

❷ To begin with, the track passed through a _____.

❸ The track came out into a _____.

❹ At the end of the valley was a _____.

D Circle SENSES for the verbs that express the act of seeing, listening, or feeling, and circle THOUGHTS for the verbs that express the act of thinking.

❶ notice SENSES THOUGHTS

❷ listen SENSES THOUGHTS

❸ guess SENSES THOUGHTS

❹ hear SENSES THOUGHTS

❺ remember SENSES THOUGHTS

❻ read SENSES THOUGHTS

Rescue

A man with a bushy beard and wire-rimmed glasses marched up and stood in front of Tara.

"What do you think you're doing?" he demanded, his cheeks flushed with rage. "Don't you know you're putting people's health at risk by wandering around out here?"

The man glanced furiously toward the row of armed security guards behind Tara.

"Would one of you care to explain how she got out of the isolation area?" he demanded.

"She must be one of the disease-resistant group; she's displaying no symptoms," said a woman with blond hair.

"Then get her back in there with them immediately," snapped the bearded man.

"They're due for antibody harvest in thirty minutes and she needs to be prepared for surgery." He reached forward and punched a number into the keypad, so the door slid open. Immediately, the guard holding Tara's arm shoved her forward so that she almost fell onto the floor.

POP QUIZ

What does "She's displaying no symptoms" mean?

ⓐ She's not showing any fear.
ⓑ She's showing no signs of illness.

KEY WORDS

- bushy
- wire-rimmed
- march up
- flush
- rage
- at risk

- wander
- furiously
- row
- armed
- guard
- care to

- -resistant
- display
- symptom
- harvest
- be due for
- surgery

Tara was dizzy and exhausted from lack of food and drink, but she pushed away the thought that really made her shiver: what was an antibody harvest, and why did she need to have surgery for it? And what would they do to her when they discovered that she wasn't supposed to be here at all? Another violent shove made her fall against a door marked *Disease Resistance Research: Live subjects.*

As she recovered her breath, the door opened and the guard waved his gun, ordering her to go through.

"If there's any funny business, you'll be the first one in line for the harvest," he said.

Tara's nose wrinkled at the strange odor of disinfectant and some sharp, vinegar scent.

A moment later, she entirely forgot about the smell as she was shown into a large room with several beds lining the walls, like a dormitory or a hospital ward. There, lying on the last bed, facing away from Tara and toward the windowless wall, was Nate. He had his back to her, but she recognized the birthmark just above his elbow, which looked like a bloody fingerprint.

POP QUIZ

How did Tara recognize Brad?
ⓐ by the bloody fingerprint on his back
ⓑ by the birthmark on his elbow

KEY WORDS

- dizzy
- lack of
- be supposed to
- violent
- subject
- recover

- funny business
- wrinkle
- odor
- sharp
- vinegar
- scent

- line
- ward
- birthmark
- fingerprint

Tara
stepped
forward,
laid a hand
on his shoulder, and whispered, "Nate?"
He turned toward her, his face half-clouded with sleep, but
suddenly, his eyes widened and he sat bolt upright.
"It *is* you, Tara!" he gasped as he leapt off the bed and folded
her into a tight, rib-crushing hug.

KEY WORDS

- half-clouded
- widen
- bolt upright

- gasp
- leap off (leap-leapt-leapt)
- fold

- rib-crushing

All of a sudden, he released her, retreated a couple of steps, and asked, "Does this mean you're infected?"

Tara shook her head, the movement making her feel so dizzy that she feared she might faint. Hopefully, now that she had been captured, someone would give her something to eat and drink.

"I'm here to... to rescue you," she murmured, swaying on her feet so that Nate had to catch hold of her just before she sank down onto the bed.

"Some rescue," he whispered, but he was grinning at the same time. "I can't believe you're here."

All Tara wanted to do was sleep, but she fought it and raised herself on her elbows. There was something she had to tell Nate—something important...

POP QUIZ

Why did Nate step back after he had hugged Tara?
ⓐ He thought she was infected.
ⓑ He was embarrassed.

KEY WORDS

- faint
- hopefully
- capture
- sway
- catch hold of
- sink down (sink-sank-sunk)

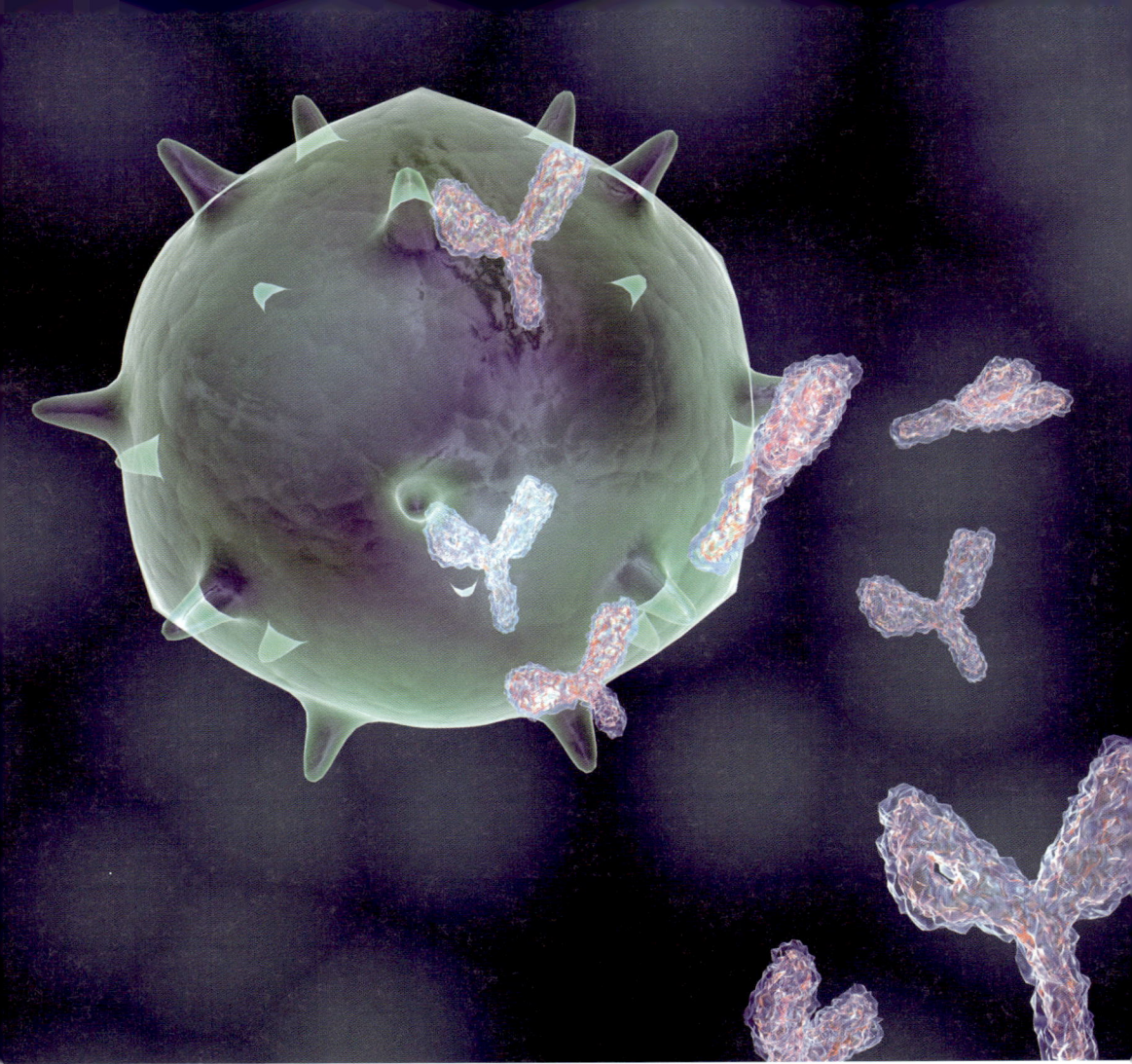

▲ antibody

"You have to get out of here," she said, shaking her head to clear the sleepy feeling. "They're going to harvest your antibodies."

Nate took her face in his warm hands and murmured, "Stay awake, Tara, and tell me what you're talking about."

Almost a dozen of their schoolmates sat around the room. Some were sleeping, some were chatting quietly, and others were pacing the room impatiently, but none of them showed any signs of poor health.

"They're all okay," she said as she pointed at them, "so why do you think they're keeping you here in isolation?"

"Because we were exposed to the disease as well," replied Nate, "but for some reason, it didn't make us ill."

"You're all resistant to it—naturally immune—and that's why they want to harvest your antibodies. (Aha!) They want to produce a new vaccine, and it's somehow linked to biological warfare. They're using you like laboratory animals."

KEY WORDS

- dozen
- clear
- stay awake
- chat
- pace
- impatiently
- point at
- be exposed to
- link

Nate's mouth fell open in astonishment. "I guess we're perfect specimens for their research. After all, what's the probability of so many kids falling ill at the same time? Since they've got all these sick kids on their hands that they're taking care of, it makes sense that they want to find out how to stop other people from getting it."

"But, Nate, you don't understand. I think they *gave* everyone the disease in the first place."

Nate's face drained of color as Tara repeated the conversation she had overheard in Mr. Lockwood's office as well as his comment about her. 📖 Aha!

"He said that I hadn't had the 'procedure,' but I don't know what he meant."

Nate slapped his palm against his forehead. "It all makes sense now that I think of it. There was one night at camp when they gave us some stew that tasted a bit... well, strange."

"Do you mean it tasted like bad meat?"

KEY WORDS

- fall open
- in astonishment
- specimen
- probability
- in the first place
- drain

- overhear
- comment
- slap (slap-slapped-slapped)
- stew
- chemical
- flavor

- bitter
- dormitory
- weird
- fast asleep

"No, more like a chemical flavor—a bitter sort of taste—so I didn't finish mine, but afterward I could barely stay awake. It was weird because kids were falling asleep at the table, and I remember one of the camp leaders picking up Brad and carrying him to his dormitory because he was fast asleep."

The mention of Brad's name made Tara lose her breath for a moment, and it was all she could do to say, "And then what happened?" 📖
Aha!

"We all somehow staggered to bed, and most of the others were snoring as soon as their heads hit their pillows."

He rubbed his eyes as though he might observe the scene better in his memory.

"But I remember... I remember some people coming in. I thought it was just a nightmare; after all, you don't normally get doctors walking into the dormitory at camp, do you?"

"What made you think they were doctors?" asked Tara, sitting up and leaning toward him.

KEY WORDS

- mention
- lose one's breath (lose-lost-lost)
- for a moment
- stagger
- snore
- observe

- in one's memory
- after all
- syringe
- inject
- ring out
- on purpose

"They were wearing white coats and carrying trays full of
syringes. They injected something into us, I'm absolutely
certain of it. I'd forgotten about it until you mentioned it just
now. It was like a dream you only remember the next time
you get into bed, but I'm sure that they must have..."
"They must have done it on purpose," said Tara, finishing
the sentence for him. "It really *was* a camp of danger."

All around the room, the conversations stopped, and silence fell as the other kids looked at her open mouthed in disbelief. "They did it on purpose!" cried Tara again, her voice rising as everything began to make sense. "They're trying to develop a biological weapon that they can use against other people, but they want to make sure our own people are protected! That's why they need to make a vaccine by using your antibodies." Nate's jaw tightened and he looked as though he wanted to punch someone.

"So that's why the government paid for everyone in school to go to the camp," he said, angrily.

"The mayor was in on the whole thing, too," agreed Tara. "They must have given him money for the town, and he told Mr. Lockwood that it was for everyone's good."

KEY WORDS

- silence
- open mouthed
- in disbelief
- protect

- jaw
- tighten
- be in on
- for one's good

- furious
- permission
- red-haired

The others moved toward her until they surrounded the bed, their faces shocked and furious.

"They can't do that without our parents' permission," declared one red-haired boy.

"They already have," said Tara, "but the question is: What are we going to do about it?"

Her eyes strayed to the clock on the wall, where the digital readout was glowing steadily.

"They'll be coming to collect us for the antibody harvest in five minutes!" she yelped.

A buzz of conversation broke out like a hive of furious wasps.

"Just be quiet, everyone!" yelled Nate, his voice slicing through the noise. "This could be our chance to escape."

Tara sighed in relief that it wasn't just her problem any longer. She lay back on the bed with her fists clenched and listened while Nate explained his plan.

KEY WORDS

- one's eyes stray to[toward]
- readout
- steadily
- collect
- yelp

- hive
- wasp
- sigh
- in relief
- slice through

- clench
- blur (blur-blurred-blurred)
- hiss

"I'll pretend that I've fallen ill," he said. "That'll confuse them, and they'll be so distracted that the rest of you will have a chance to…"

His voice became distant, blurring in Tara's mind with the hum of the overhead fan that stirred the air. She was thinking about another problem: Where was Brad, and how was she supposed to get him out of here? Even as she was about to mention it to Nate, the door slid open with a hiss, and the bearded man stood there with two armed guards.

"What's going on here?" he demanded. "You were all told to rest, not to gather around and have a party."

"But he's sick, sir," said the red-haired boy, pointing at Nate, who had dropped to the floor and was clutching his stomach.

"He can't be," muttered the bearded man, elbowing his way through the group and crouching beside Nate. "His blood tests show that he's got natural immunity."

After a short pause, during which he lifted Nate's eyelids and took his pulse, he snapped at the guards, "Take the other nine."

Tara gasped, rolled off the bed, and dropped into the gap on the other side. She hoped they wouldn't notice her.

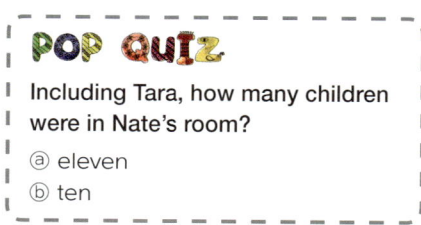

POP QUIZ

Including Tara, how many children were in Nate's room?
ⓐ eleven
ⓑ ten

KEY WORDS

- rest
- clutch
- elbow
- pause
- eyelid

- snap at
- gasp
- gap
- haul
- gritted

- unsuitable
- definitely
- extra

"There are ten, sir," said one of the guards as he reached into the gap and hauled Tara out, which sent a sharp pain through her shoulder.

"I know there are ten," said the bearded man through gritted teeth, "but this one is unsuitable for harvest, so take the other nine."

"I mean there are ten *as well as* the boy," insisted the guard, counting again under his breath. "This one here is definitely one extra."

Tara's gaze flickered toward the open door and then rested on Nate, who nodded slightly. She stamped hard on the guard's foot, and, at the same time, drove her elbow into his stomach. Twisting in his arms, she managed to struggle free and dived toward the door. The guard leapt after her, but the red-haired boy launched himself across the room with a screech and knocked him to the floor.

At the same moment, Nate sprang up, pushed the bearded man aside, and drove his fist into the second guard's chin. As everyone stampeded toward the door, they knocked down the first guard, who was just struggling to get up. They poured into the corridor with Tara at the front and Nate bringing up the rear.

"Which way?" she yelled.

"I was hoping you would know," Nate called back. His voice was almost drowned by the sudden shriek of a siren.

Tara knew that she hadn't passed any doors on the way that looked as though sick people were behind them, which meant that Brad and the others were further down.

KEY WORDS

- one's gaze[eyes] flicker toward(s)
- rest on
- stamp
- at the same time
- dive (dive-dived/dove-dived)
- launch
- screech

- spring up (spring-sprang-sprung)
- stampede
- bring up the rear
- drowned
- shriek
- further

Although every instinct told her to escape, to find her way back to the loading bay and to try to smash through the outer doors, she couldn't bring herself to do it. Her brother was in here somewhere. He was sick and frightened, and without his mom. Tara was not leaving without him.

"That way," she ordered, pointing the way she had come as the other kids streamed past her, a wave of bodies and drumming feet.

Nate was the last one to pass. As he went by, Tara darted in the opposite direction. Nate spun around. He hung back as the others raced toward the exit, despite the appearance around the corner of several rows of guards.

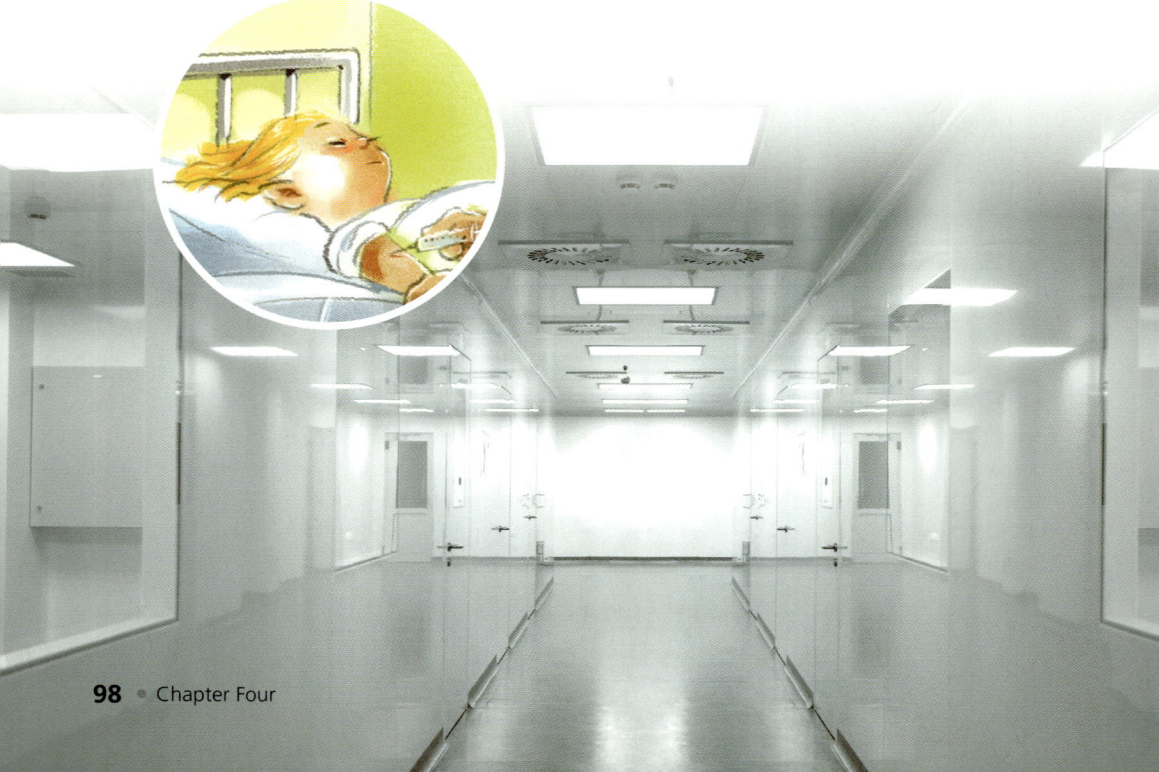

"Where do you think you're going?" he hissed.

"I have to get Brad," she replied.

Without hesitating, Nate simply nodded, grabbed her arm, and pulled her along until they reached the next door that blocked the corridor. On it was an even more threatening notice, warning that nobody should enter without protective clothing and breathing equipment. 📖 Tara thought about all the unpleasant diseases that could be waiting to infect her beyond that barrier, but this was no time to worry about them.

KEY WORDS

- instinct
- loading bay
- smash through
- cannot bring oneself to
- somewhere
- stream
- direction
- spin around (spin-span-spun)
- hang back
- appearance
- nod
- barrier

KEY WORDS

- get in
- code
- contain
- fire alarm
- in case of

- emergency
- operate
- instantly
- make one's decision
- deafening

- sprinkler
- unnoticed
- chaos

"How do we get in?" said Nate urgently. "Do you know the code for the keypad?"

But Tara had noticed something fixed to the wall: a small glass box that contained a large green button.

"It's a fire alarm," she murmured to herself as she read the words on the box. "In case of emergency, break glass."

Next to it was a map of the building that showed all the electronically operated doors.

Instantly making her decision, Tara drove her elbow into the glass and gasped as broken pieces cut her skin. At once, another deafening siren sounded, adding to the noise, and sprinklers began to shower water from the ceiling. The lights went off, leaving only the pale, blue glow of emergency lights dotted along the corridor. It wasn't much, but it was enough to see that, unnoticed in the chaos, the electronic door had slid open.

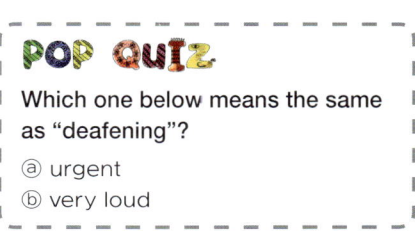

POP QUIZ

Which one below means the same as "deafening"?

ⓐ urgent
ⓑ very loud

Tara dashed into the room, which was very similar to the one Nate had been held captive in. Here, the beds were full of humped shapes, and the odor of sickness filled the air.

"We can't get them all out!" yelled Nate. "We'll get help and come back for them."

But Tara gritted her teeth and tried to block out the smell. She went from bed to bed, peeled back the bed covers, and peered at the faces beneath. At last, she heard a faint groan coming from a bed halfway down the room.

Tara rushed toward it and saw the familiar shape of her brother's face against the white pillow.

KEY WORDS

- dash into
- hold captive
- hump
- peel

- at last
- halfway
- all bones and angles
- light

- watchful
- urge

"Is that you, Mom?" he whispered, holding out his arms to her. "No, but I'll take you to her," said Tara, trying not to cry as she lifted Brad from the bed, all bones and angles, and much lighter than she remembered. Nate, alert and watchful in the corridor, urged her to hurry.

POP QUIZ

Why was Brad so much lighter than Tara remembered?

ⓐ He had lost weight because of his illness.
ⓑ Tara was stronger than she used to be.

Tara struggled out into the corridor with Brad in her arms and almost slipped on the floor, which was now covered with water.

"There they are!" shouted the bearded man.

He stood a few meters away and pointed accusingly at them. His face was almost purple with rage. There was no time now to worry about diseases.

It seemed impossible that the noise could get any louder, but above the shriek of the alarms, Tara heard the *thwock-thwock* of helicopter blades. Then, the floor heaved, and the walls shook as the force of an explosion blasted half the ceiling away. Terrified, Tara held Brad to her chest as several men wearing black clothes came down on ropes and landed on the floor in front of her.

One of them grabbed Tara and asked, "Are you hurt, miss?" She gasped for breath and shook her head, but before she could answer properly, the man nodded and raced away to join the others down the corridor.

KEY WORDS

- **slip** (slip-slipped-slipped)
- **accusingly**
- **blade**
- **explosion**

- **blast**
- **land**
- **gasp for breath**

Suddenly, the sirens stopped, revealing the sound of thuds and agonized yelps. The water stopped pouring from the sprinklers, and all the lights came on, showing the devastation in the corridor.  One of the men returned, stripped off his mask, and flashed some kind of identity card in front of Tara.

"Special forces," he announced while breathing heavily. "You're safe now."

"But who..." gasped Nate. "How did you know...?"

"Where's Lockwood?" shouted the man to someone down the corridor. "You should be able to find him with the tracking device."

POP QUIZ

Circle two words which mean the same as *devastation*.

damage   excitement   device   destruction

KEY WORDS

- agonize
- devastation
- strip off (strip-stripped-stripped)
- flash
- identity card

- special forces
- tracking device
- military police
- signal

Mr. Lockwood had a *tracking device*? It was something that would allow the military police to follow its signal and to find out exactly where he was. An image of the watch with the blinking red light flashed into Tara's memory. So that was what he had meant when he said he would do something about it.

Tara's knees felt suddenly weak. She still hadn't eaten, and she had been running on excitement and fear for hours. The man in black caught her and gently lifted Brad out of her arms.

"There are more sick kids in there," she said, nodding toward the hospital ward.

"They did it on purpose. They infected everyone so that they could make a vaccine and…"

"…and make a lot of money," finished the man. His voice was angry, but his eyes were kind.

"We know all about it. We suspected something was going on, but we had no information about the location of their laboratory until your principal, brave man that he is, offered to try to get in."

KEY WORDS

- excitement
- suspect
- location
- regard
- with a steady gaze
- indeed
- overflow with
- nowhere near

Tara slid slowly to the floor and let her head fall back against
the wall. She took deep, sobbing breaths of relief that it was
all over. Brad would get better, and everyone could go home.
Nate crouched in front of her and took her hands in his own.
He regarded her with a steady gaze.

"He is indeed a brave man," he said, his voice overflowing
with pride, "but nowhere near as brave as my Tara."

Chapter Four

Comprehension Quiz

A Which character would say these lines? Write the name of the character in each blank.

Tara　　*Bearded man*　　*Guard*　　*Nate*

❶ Why is this boy ill? His blood tests show that he should be healthy. _____

❷ When can I get some food and sleep? _____

❸ Why did our food taste strange at the school camp?

_____

❹ Why is there an extra person hiding behind the bed?

_____

B Mark T for true or F for false.

❶ The bearded man carried a gun. ☐T ☐F

❷ The scientists gave Tara an injection. ☐T ☐F

❸ The scientists injected the children at the camp with germs. ☐T ☐F

❹ The children's parents gave permission for them to be injected. ☐T ☐F

C Choose the best answer to each question.

❶ Why were all the children in Nate's room healthy?

a) They were immune to the disease.

b) They had not been injected with the disease.

c) They had not been at the school camp.

d) They were from a different school.

❷ How had Mr. Lockwood led the military men to find him?

a) He had called the newspapers.

b) He had a tracking device hidden in his watch.

c) He had signaled with a flashing light.

d) He had left a trail of footprints.

D Put the sentences in order.

❶ The red-haired boy knocked the guard to the floor.

❷ Nate pushed the bearded man aside.

❸ Everyone went out into the corridor.

❹ Nate pretended he was ill.

❺ Tara dived toward the door.

❻ Tara stamped on the guard's foot.

_____ → _____ → _____ → _____ → _____ → _____

Let's Review the Story

Fill in the blanks to review the story.

❶ Title: [_____]

❷ Main Characters (3): [_____] , [_____] , [_____]

❸ Other Characters: [_____] , [_____] , [_____] ,
[_____] , [_____] , [_____] , [_____]

❹ Problem: All the kids that go to the [_____] [_____] come
back ill. [_____] and Nate are taken away into isolation.
[_____] wants to get them back, but she doesn't know [_____]
[_____] [_____] or how to r[_____] [_____] .

❺ Solution 1: [_____] gets onto the MedLabX [_____] ,
which takes her to the [_____] where the [_____] are.
But she still doesn't know how to find [_____] and [_____] ,
and there is the danger that she will be i[_____] , too.

❻ Solution 2: Tara finds [_____] .
But now she is a p[_____] , too, and she must have s[_____]
to [_____] her a[_____] . She still doesn't know where
[_____] is.

❼ Final Solution: Tara finds [_____] . She sets off the [_____]
[_____] to open all the [_____] . Some m[_____] men
arrive since they followed Mr. Lockwood's [_____] [_____] .
The children can go h[_____] .

Let's Think & Talk

Think about the following questions and answer them freely.

❶ Microorganisms are tiny creatures that you only can see under the microscope. Tell us what roles these microorganisms play in nature.

❷ If viruses that cause disease such as a cold float around the air, what action should we take so that they won't come into our body and make us sick?

❸ Explain why some of your friends catch a cold, while others don't?

❹ Medical experiments on humans are an inhumane act that we mustn't do. But they actually have happened throughout history. Talk about them if you know when and what happened.

Let's Review the Story

❶ Title: A Trip to Camp Danger

❷ Main Characters (3): Tara , Nate , Brad

❸ Other Characters: Mr. Lockwood , the mayor , the bearded man ,
Mom , Dad , soldiers , Nate's neighbors

❹ Problem: All the kids that go to the school camp come
back ill. Brad and Nate are taken away into isolation.
Tara wants to get them back, but she doesn't know where
they are or how to rescue them .

❺ Solution 1: Tara gets onto the MedLabX van ,
which takes her to the cavern where the laboratories are.
But she still doesn't know how to find Brad and Nate ,
and there is the danger that she will be infected , too.

❻ Solution 2: Tara finds Nate .
But now she is a prisoner , too, and she must have surgery
to harvest her antibodies . She still doesn't know where
Brad is.

❼ Final Solution: Tara finds Brad . She sets off the fire
alarm to open all the doors . Some military men
arrive since they followed Mr. Lockwood's tracking device .
The children can go home .

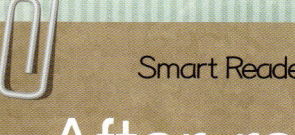

Smart Readers: **Wise & Wide**

After-reading **Test**

- A Trip to Camp Danger
- Level 6
- 29 Questions

(Vocabulary 7 / Reading Comprehension 16 /

Sentence Structure & Grammar 6)

1. Which of the following has the similar meaning with the word "entire"?
   ① high   ② elementary
   ③ whole   ④ old

2. Which of the following has the similar meaning with the word "haste"?
   ① hurry   ② fear
   ③ operate   ④ rest

3. Which of the following does NOT have the similar meaning with the word "smell"?
   ① odor   ② sweet
   ③ fragrance   ④ scent

※ Choose the right word for each blank. (4~5)

4.
   > Tara _____ a hand on Brad's forehead in Brad's bedroom.

   ① laid   ② lay
   ③ lie   ④ lain

5.
   > Mr. Lockwood _____ his broad, bald head with a large handkerchief.

   ① cleared   ② wore
   ③ wiped   ④ folded

※ Choose the common word for the two blanks. (6~7)

6.
> • The beds were full _____ humped shapes.
> • Tara saw the familiar face _____ her
>   brother on the pillow.

① on   ② of   ③ with   ④ off

7.
> • Tara imagined the virus _____ a tiny,
>   spiky bomb.
> • Tara stumbled _____ she crept toward the
>   glow in the cavern.

① into   ② for   ③ so   ④ as

8. Which statement is true?
   ① Tara had been looking forward to being ill.
   ② Mom and Dad had paid for the school camp.
   ③ Only Brad's class were going to camp.
   ④ Brad did not wash his hair while he was away.

9. Why was Mr. Lockwood wiping his head with a handkerchief?
   ① It was raining outside.
   ② He had just taken a shower.
   ③ He was sweating because he was worried.
   ④ He did not want to get infected.

10. Why did Tara give the man Brad's teddy?
   ① She thought that it was infected.
   ② She thought that it might comfort Brad.
   ③ She thought she had to give him all of Brad's things.
   ④ She thought it might help her to find Brad later.

11. "Let him go with us, or we'll deliver the full charge," threatened one of the men. What did he mean?
　① Nate would have to make a payment.
　② Nate had committed a crime.
　③ Pete had committed a crime.
　④ He was going to put electricity through Nate's body.

12. Why had Tara never noticed the noise other children made until it was gone?
　① She couldn't hear very well.
　② The children played quietly.
　③ She was used to the sound.
　④ She never played with other children.

13. Where did the "messages of hate" come from?
　① the mayor
　② parents whose children had been taken away
　③ Nate's neighbor
　④ Nate's brother Pete

14. Why were the mayor and Mr. Lockwood arguing?
　① They both wanted a share of the money from the government.
　② The mayor thought that Mr. Lockwood ran the school badly.
　③ Mr. Lockwood thought that the mayor ran the town badly.
　④ Mr. Lockwood thought that the children should not have been taken away.

15. What was the MedLabX research program about?
　① finding ways to make money for the mayor
　② finding ways to make new vaccines
　③ finding ways to make medicine for animals
　④ finding ways to cure people who had been injured in a war

16. Why does the author describe Tara as "an athlete at the start of a race"?
    ① She was very fit and healthy.
    ② She had very large muscles.
    ③ She was prepared for sudden action.
    ④ She could run faster than a moving vehicle.

17. What is a restricted zone?
    ① an area where only certain people are allowed to go
    ② an area that is open to everyone
    ③ a narrow space that is difficult to get into
    ④ a scientific laboratory where experiments are carried out

18. Why did Tara crawl in the corridor?
    ① She was feeling too ill to stand.
    ② She hoped that the camera wouldn't see her.
    ③ She was feeling tired and weak.
    ④ She thought it might stop from her catching germs.

19. Why did Tara decide to go down the Protozoa corridor?
    ① She couldn't remember learning about them.
    ② She knew that protozoa caused the symptoms that Brad had.
    ③ She made a random guess.
    ④ She was being chased by scientists.

20. Why were the healthy children going to have surgery?
    ① to make them ill
    ② to remove some body parts
    ③ to remove some of their antibodies to make vaccines
    ④ to make them look different

21. Why did Tara ignore the threatening notice about protective clothing and breathing equipment?
    ① She wasn't worried about the danger.
    ② She couldn't read the notice.
    ③ She didn't understand the notice.
    ④ She wanted to find Brad despite the danger.

22. Why did Tara decide to set off the fire alarm?
    ① She thought that the corridor was on fire.
    ② She thought that all the electronic doors would be unlocked.
    ③ She wanted to cause a flood.
    ④ She wanted to make a loud noise.

23. Why was Tara so weak at the end of the story?
    ① She was infected with the disease.
    ② She had been given an injection.
    ③ She hadn't eaten or drunk anything for a long time.
    ④ She'd had surgery to remove her antibodies.

※ Choose the wrong part of each sentence. (24~25)

24.
The water stopped to pour from the sprinklers,
         ①   ②

and all the lights came on.
       ③   ④

25.
I wish you are coming to Camp Danger with me.
 ①   ②   ③   ④

※ Choose the correct word or phrase for each blank. (26~27)

26.
I've got to go, _____ I'll miss the bus.

① and   ② or   ③ but   ④ so

27.
Why does _____ the flu make me so hot?

① having   ② have   ③ had   ④ having done

※ Choose the correct sentence. (28~29)

28. ① She was looking half asleep.
    ② She is look half asleep.
    ③ She is looked half asleep.
    ④ She looked half asleep.

29. ① The tiled floor was very clean that it almost dazzled her to look at it.
    ② The tiled floor was so clean that it almost dazzled her to look at it.
    ③ The tiled floor has cleaned that it almost dazzled her to look at it.
    ④ The tiled floor was too cleaning that it almost dazzled her to look at it.

Memo

Memo

Memo

Memo

Sarah J. Dodd

Sarah J. Dodd is an experienced primary school teacher who resides in the UK, but has also taught in Australia. She has a PhD in Science and a certificate in Creative Writing. She has published four books for younger children — 'An Angel Anyway' (Anyway Press) and the Little Angels' series (Lion Hudson plc). Her children's Bible will be published in 2015. She is currently working on a novel for 9-12 year olds and another for young adults.

Smart Readers
Wise & Wide **6-1**

A Trip to Camp Danger

Written by Sarah J. Dodd
Illustrated by Yeseon Cho

First Published in December 2014

Editorial Manager: Juyon Choi
Editors: Juyon Choi, Jeeyoung Kim, Kyunghee Jang, Jiyeong Park
Designers: Eunhee Lee, Elim
Cover Designer: Eunhee Lee

Published and distributed by

Happy House

Darakwon Bldg., 64-1 Jandari-ro, Mapo-gu, Seoul, Korea 121-894
Tel: 82-2-736-2031(ext. 250)   Fax: 82-2-736-2037
Homepage: www.ihappyhouse.co.kr
Publisher: Kyudo Chung

ISBN: 978-89-6653-170-7 18740 / 978-89-6653-156-1 18740(set)

[Components]
• 1 Audio CD (Recording Studio: Aram)
• Answer Keys & Korean Translation: Free download at www.ihappyhouse.co.kr